For Crying Out Loud

Poems by

Kitty Fitzgerald
Valerie Laws

IRON
PRESS

First published 1994 by IRON Press
5 Marden Terrace, Cullercoats
North Shields, Northumberland NE30 4PD
Tel: 091–253 1901

Typeset by Roger Booth Associates
10 Bigg Market, Newcastle upon Tyne
in Bookman Light 10 point

Printed by Peterson Printers, South Shields

Supported by Northern Arts

© Kitty Fitzgerald and Valerie Laws, 1994

ISBN 0 906228 49 2

IRON Press books
are represented & distributed by
Password Books Ltd
23 New Mount Street
Manchester M4 4DE
Tel: 061–953 4009
Fax: 061–953 4001

Kitty Fitzgerald

Valerie Laws

– Kitty Fitzgerald –

KITTY FITZGERALD was born in Ireland in 1946 but came to live in England as a child. After leaving school at fifteen, she did a variety of jobs, including waitressing, shop work, factory work, until she went to college as a mature student in 1976. She taught Art before starting to write seriously in 1982 when her first short story was published. After writing residencies with the Sikh Family History Project in Manchester and Bradford & Ilkley Adult Literary Centre, she came to Tyneside in 1986 to take up a writer's residency in Gateshead and stayed. Between 1988 and 1993 she was a member of Amber Films Workshop and between 1991 and 1993 an assistant editor of IRON magazine. She has a grown-up daughter and two grandsons.

Also by Kitty Fitzgerald

Fiction
'Marge', a novel. *Sheba*, 1985
'Tight Corners', short stories, *Portcullis*, 1987

Film
'A Clearing in the Woods', Channel 4, 1983. (Director) Documentary
'Shields Stories', Amber Films 1987. Drama series
'Dream On', Amber Films, 1991. Feature

Theatre
'Break My Bones', winner of the *Next Stage* Playwriting Award, 1992
'Fox', Durham Theatre Company, 1993
'Where Or When', Durham Theatre Company, 1993

Radio
'Grandma and Mrs Chatterjee', BBC Radio 4, 1993

Her poetry has been published in *IRON; The Wide Skirt; Eight 'til Late; What big eyes you've got; The Common Thread; Pennine Magazine; Tight Corners* and *Newcastle Evening Chronicle.*

The Sea

It comes and comes
like a favourite lover
filling every
cockled crevice
till the tide turns
and the sand sighs
a long breath
before calling it back.

The Crusades

If you don't
convert voluntarily;
call a halt
to those rituals
in praise of sex;
adopt our
commandments;
walk in fear
of the Lord;
stop painting
your loins
with the tinted wax
of honey bees
and your breasts
with oil of heather;
get on your knees
to say your prayers
instead of dancing;
stop those youths
who dress as women
leading processions
on our Holy Days;
kiss the Bishop's hand
without complaining,
even though it's
covered with
enormous warts;
take one husband
only, even if he
turns into a bore;
stop your children
lifting up my frock
coat, to see if I'm a man;

If you don't,
your festivals
will be banned,
your temples crushed,
your priestess burned,
your carvings
turned to dust.
In the name of
the Father, the Son
and the Holy Ghost.

Wolf
(with thanks to Clarissa Pinkola Estes)

I am wolf
nurtured
on sheep lies
darkness hides nothing
from my lupine eyes,
don't push me too far.

I'm fluent
in the language of dreams
there's passion in my pores,
you'll find telltale signs
of wet footprints and
long coarse hairs
on your pillow and floor
if you push me too far.

You've seen my coloured ribbons
lying everywhere,
did you think they were
to tame my hair?
You've heard my voice
when twilight comes,
sighing to the rhythm
of unseen drums.
I am wolf
under this skin
don't lick me too hard
or the change will begin.

Rolling in leaf drifts
the pack moves soft and near,
mist of civet, musk
and scent of deer.
I can howl
at journey's end,
I will bite
betraying friends.
My back begins
its bending
if you push me too far.

Seahorse
(for Peter)

After you left
I found your earring
in my bed,
that seahorse
with the jet inset.
It glinted in the
morning sun
recalling your
fingertips
on the back
of my knees.

I'd like to hibernate with you,
curl up around smooth firm limbs
amidst stockpiles of cheese and fruit,
wake up lustful, lick your face,
pull you tumbling
around our dusky cave,
savour the feel of skin on skin,
sleep and begin again.

There's too much
fitting in otherwise.
Thoughts of thighs
get squeezed between
targets, meetings,
an accumulation
of daily deadlines.

The seahorse hangs
in my ear now,
tickling the hairs
on my neck,
treading water
till you come back.

Neighbours

He sat day by day routinely placed
beneath his union apprenticeship certificate
which hung like a large reminder
of where he'd been

back bent, toenails grown in, eyes
still blue in their watery sockets
he told me boilermaker's tales
about the railway company
which took him on, how it shunted
him back and forth, a slight lad
with proud step measured
by the piece rate

the only fresh air he felt
for ten years flickered or
gusted about his
zimmerframed body
on its slow tread in and out
to the lavatory

indoors, gas fire turned low
spluttering like his breath
I poured oil on his joints
from a hand made can
filled with multigrade

I was amazed at his resilience
at his ninety years of pain
for he was rarely happy
he said

one wintry morning just before dawn
woken by the rattle of his door
I rose shivering from my bed
snowflakes tickled my cheeks as
I fumbled with icy letterbox and key
to find him struck down,
speechless,
he died

few relatives attended his funeral
but we wore black and sang
unfamiliar tearful hymns in that barren
place where we hoped he lay
at rest

afterwards, by his dustbin,
we found sepia photos of a young man
laughing warmly between the Wars.

Only Joking

I didn't really mean it
when I said I'd
pickle your prick
in toxic waste.
I was reacting
to your comments
on my nipples
and to the thought
of all those other women
you said you fancied
more than me.
I haven't got
an illicit supply
of morphine
which will send you to
the land of Nod
while I don my
surgical gloves
and cover the walls
with polythene.
Where's your
sense of humour?
Can't we rewind
the previous hour
and pretend
you never said
my backside sags
or the bags
under my eyes
are bursting
at the seams?
I mean it darling.
Of course I can
take a joke.

Here, drink your tea
it's a new blend
from the delicatessen.
Careful or you'll spill it,
don't want to
stain the carpet
unnecessarily.
Yes, I know you're sorry
you lied about sleeping
with Ann and Sonia
without using condoms.
You're feeling tired
are you? Well,
just drink up, lie back
and think of England's
chances in the Nations Cup.

Aquatic Apes
(with thanks to Elaine Morgan)

Sometimes I feel
a filigree of web
between my toes
tickling a memory
of centuries of sea.
Clear ocean landscapes
recall sweet lusts
and babies born with fins.

Like whales
did we escape
our predators
by entering the sea?
Is that why we're drawn
lemming-like
to sea and sand,
yearning for an
aquatic past?

Floating belly up
sky patterns map out
a sort of history.
Swimming is a legend,
stories unfold as my ears
lie beneath your surface
listening to spells.

Will you swallow
your offspring one day,
before they destroy
your amniotic well
with their leftovers?

Battering

He keeps coming back,
carrion pigeon,
withering her conviction
wounding her inside out.

His fists tattoo her dreams,
grave warnings,
there's no place to go
while he walks free.

Some say she is
a willing victim,
thriving on the drama;
others, that she asks

for every stitch that
puckers the skin he's broken
repeatedly.
All she ever wanted

was romance; the stuff
of fifties' movies,
cigarette drooping from
her Jane Russell lips.

Teatimes With You
(for Mum)

On Sunday afternoons
I slyly serve
Carnation milk and
tinned peaches
to my grandsons,
more used to pizza
and ice cream,
so that I can re-live
teatimes with you.

Gingham tablecloths
and matching plates,
your square hands
always smelling faintly
of raw onions.

We'd come back steaming
from long walks,
dad would go to work
on his correspondence course
in Public Speaking.
Father Dorsey would call
on his rusty bike
to debate again
the nature of faith;
you and I would hear
the lift and lilt
of their voices
through the wall
as we sang along
to the radio.

You gave me strength
to swim against the tide
although you liked to
hide my behaviour
from the neighbours.

Mum, I will always
paint my bathroom red;
welcome wild lovers in my bed
(but never want to marry them)
and encourage my grandsons
to dream dangerous dreams
as I serve them peaches and cream.

Pit Man

He'd dug up coal for many a year
his lungs told me so,
rasping like a concrete mixer.
Blue scars lined his face
signalling where he'd been
enlisted fresh from school.
There's no malice in his tale
of seams no higher
than my knees.
No bitterness lines his tongue
about the violence done
to colliers.
And he laughs still
at the memory of
spat-clad Bevin Boys
while he coughs up blood.

South American Miners

They make them wear
hard plastic copies
of old chastity belts
to stop them stuffing
diamonds up their arse.
Hauling tubs like donkeys
up gravelly hillsides,
mud oozes from their pores.
In snapshots
they look like
red-earth statues,
hundreds of them
lining the hostile ground
like termites drugged
with laudanum.
Production is up
one hundred percent
General Sanchez says,
backhanders
propping up his
syphillitic frame
since the coca cola
bottles came.

I Can't Help It

I know I shouldn't
I know it's wrong
I know my mum would blush with shame
and lay the blame on TV
if she knew.
I'm an eighties' gal
I've read the right books
but my friends would shout with rage
and blame the age of chauvinism.
I don't remember when it started
I don't recall the day
but my husband surely never knew
or he'd certainly go blue with fury.
Blue, blue, that washed-out blue
of the denim crotch
where bunches of ripe plums
nestle for me to watch.
I am unashamed
but I am particular
about which side I'm on:
I prefer men who hang to the left.

Johnny

Johnny was short when it was great to be tall
his teeth fought for space in a mouth too small
his nose was crooked and longer than most
he joked that it was good for detecting burning toast.

None of the girls loved Johnny; let's be friends they said,
but friends don't stroke your thighs at dawn
or tell you secrets in bed; their eyes
don't shine when they smile at you
and you know what's going on in their head.

What a dancer Johnny was, feet like magic slippers;
twirling, gliding, twisting; making his partners breathless.
He danced all night, was never refused,
for the fast jive numbers girls formed a queue.
The touch of bodies, the scent of perfume,
the glow of enjoyment, the admiration in the room.

At the bus stop later he stood alone, listening
to the laughter, the whispers, the groans.
Friends last forever, lovers come and may soon go,
an acquaintance said, when Johnny was feeling low.
Johnny didn't want eternity, or gentleness or affection,
he wanted passion, no matter how brief.
He wanted love, not courtesy.

At thirty five Johnny killed himself
in his tiny gas-filled room.
A note left on his shelf said:
Please, dance on my tomb.
And on his sixties' jacket with its
narrow silk lapels, he wore his jiving medals
for his last farewell.

Going Back

Each year, on the cattle boat,
immune to the mischievous
rocking of the sea with its
tales of treachery and
whispers heard at gravesides,
I went home to visit.

Crisp Autumn evenings,
fanning the flames
in the walk-in fireplace
until the wheel which
turned the belt blurred
like a distant firework,
I absorbed your stories
through my open mouth.

Grandad shot by Black & Tans;
guns stacked on my mother's cot;
the fairy ring disturbed
by Connor's spade, poultices
made from goat dung
to halt his raving;
banshees, ghosts
with purple eyes,
spies from the government
riding British bikes.

Ageing sorceress
in dark flowered pinafores,
the weight of your
disappointments
could have crushed
a continent.
But you brushed
my mind with magic
and kept me coming back.

Voices

I come from generations
of illiterate women
whose tales were told,
not on paper
but in the lilt of a song
or among fireside company
when a long working day was done.

Those are the voices
I carry within me,
shades of greenery
from field and plough,
red knuckles twisting watery sheets
in sunshine, frost and snow,
scratched legs from gathering peat.

You say they're valueless
as a tradition,
to work from and build
onto inch by inch,
you say their songs and tales
are nothing more important
than the echo of a banshee wail.

I cannot take you seriously,
there is no spirit
nor any magic
in the tongue of history
you insist on lashing.
Go back to your mother's knee
and hear herstory.

Dad

In O'Mara's caff in Dublin,
rain splattered
the greasy window panes;
flies played hockey
with the crumbs
on the table;
papers with sticky corpses
hung like tropical vines,
as I heard you say
you were going away.
I learnt my first lesson then
looking at your charcoal eyes
which seemed to throw
a challenge down.

At the dockside I clamped on to you
locking arms and legs like rat's teeth,
beneath your smile
you knew you'd have to
batter me to death to get free.
Mam waited, this wasn't her war,
I was strong but I was only four.
When the boat left without you
the sun came out.

You taught me to take risks
you made me strong
I grew bolder
listening to your songs.
Words you gave me
weave into my schemes:
'Never turn your anger inwards,
it will mangle your dreams.'
O'Mara's caff is gone now,
just like you,
flypapers swept aside
by lights fluorescent blue,
part of me still living
part of you.

Jonathon Harker's Recipes

Jonathon, there's something
curious about this recipe
you sent via Budapest,
the bitter taste
made Lucy retch;
small white crystals
poured onto her plate
like malignant salts;
blood spurted from her nose
despite the tea of aloes.

Are you sure about
the horse's urine?
It was a mare
of the highest stock
but my Sunday frock
was ruined when it spilt;
filling the banana skins
with acorns soaked
in chicken blood
caused quite a fuss with cook!

Mina, darling girl,
the Count assures me
all is well, as well can be
with his ancient family recipe.
It was designed specifically
to cleanse the system
thoroughly, to make
the heart beat as it should,
swell the delicate arteries
and purify the blood.

Lucy is so anaemic
it must have made
her system work too fast.
Last night the Count
revealed he had a need
for extra blood himself.
Imagine that my little sweet:
the Count and Lucy meeting,
their pale pale faces joined as one,
their pale pale veins a-beating.

Great Expectations

I came to find you
in the late afternoon
soft strong thighs
pressing into my thoughts
I caught you undressed
with the woman next door
tumbling and rolling
all over the floor
your bum looked so silly
sticking up in the air
and those varicose veins
didn't know they were there
I started to laugh
as my anger subsided
your erection went limp
you attempted to hide it
all I've remembered
of your body since then
are the bumps on your backside
like a badly plucked hen.

Mission Completed

Don't turn away
when your orgasm comes,
at this stage your face
is more interesting
than your bum.

Runners don't stop
the second they cross the line
I'm sure if you try
you can give me
a bit more time.

Your ejaculation
isn't necessarily
my gratification,
so use your imagination
to give me compensation.

Parting

Parting can be like a feather
floating in a stream, or waking
from a terribly unhappy dream;
a relief, a sigh, or, like with us
a long sharp anguished cry.

What we have lost
is not in the past,
that holds true,
but on that leafy
sun-filled road,
the sky so blue,
that now will never
welcome me and you.

Something is stuck in a crevice
on that sighing sand.
One All Souls night, will it fly,
abandoning its natural fear,
into a night both feverish and clear?

Autumn

Not for me the sweaty
crotch of summer
or the limpid lull
of winter chill,
Springtime can be okay
but give me Autumn any day.

Not for me the ritzy
smell of sun oil
or the vaseline
for frosty skin,
moisturiser's here to stay
but give me Autumn any day.

July bleaches out the colours,
January makes them blue,
there's a clarity in May
but give me Autumn any day.

Not for me a death
amid a heatwave
or a cold and icy
funeral day, maybe
I wouldn't mind
a snowdrop wreath
but dig my grave
upon an Autumn day.

Let me die among the falling leaves,
ruby, amber, saffron, mauve.
My heart was never comfortable with grey
since I was born upon an Autumn day.

Raj

She had known a sun
hotter than I cared to imagine,
lived mostly out of doors
had six kids by
the age of twenty four.
We interviewed each other
across an old school desk,
pockmarked with memories
of Empire Days.
Kohl-lined eyes on
cinnamon silk skin
highlighted my
Celtic pallor.
Her head tossed
occasionally
wafting the scent
of Jasmine to
mingle with my
Sandalwood wrists.

Short 'n' Curlies

Nellie had worked in all the wards
plus seven years in Casualty
and ten in Nose & Throat.
Shaving pubic hair off
had been a regular task
but not once in thirty years
had she heard a woman ask
about the size of her vagina
was it small or was it large
was it bigger than her neighbours
or just merely average
did it matter about depth
or was width the crucial bit
would it satisfy her lovers
or leave them feeling miffed?

Love Song

He wanted to possess me
so he played hard to get
and I left.
He wanted me to
darn his socks,
when he went to the pub
I changed the door locks.
He put me on
a pedestal,
insisting I be pure,
I couldn't endure it.
He said I should
be faithful
while he
screwed around
so I left town.
But you have
filled me up
without displacing
any part of me.
I feel enclosed
yet still entirely free.

– Valerie Laws –

VALERIE LAWS is an English graduate, who taught until disabled in 1986. She is now a best-selling author of modern language textbooks and studying for a degree in Maths and Astrophysics. She lives in her native Whitley Bay with her husband and two children, has also lived in Pembrokeshire, Snowdonia, London, and a Norman castle in the Forest of Dean. She has been widely published in magazines and anthologies, has broadcast on local BBC radio, was a prizewinner in National Poetry Competition 1990 and in the Evening Chronicle/Bloodaxe competition two years running, and recently became Reviews Editor of IRON Magazine. She is fanatical about swimming.

Acknowledgements

Thirteen of these poems have previously appeared in the following publications:

Odyssey, IRON, Fat Chance, Outposts, Bound Spiral, Newcastle Evening Chronicle, Poetry Marathon '93. 'Mrs Kirk' was a fourth prizewinner in the National Poetry Competition 1990. 'Bell-buoy' and 'Toothache' were prizewinners in the Bloodaxe/Evening Chronicle competition 1989 and 1990, respectively.

Don't Put Your Daughter into Space, Mrs Kirk

What happens to old spacewomen? Or even, slightly middle aged?
In the future of equal opportunities, no job is closed to women
(save Captain).
They rocket up, chief this, commander that,
while barely in their twenties; heads,
we presume, full of micro-circuits, they sway
the shining corridors of starships, in skin-tight catsuits.

But while the men, of varying handsomeness, spread, go grey,
and dare to baldly go where no woman has before
(towards an old age pension)
they disappear. Sent home perhaps to breed
their brains and beauty into future crews,
or jettisoned in hyper-space, like garbage.
Perhaps beamed down to some obscure planet, to join
a crowd of aging women with degrees in astro-physics
discovering the joy of leaving their mascara off.

It must be hard to save the ship from aliens, all the while
waiting for the signal to drop out of active service,
being no longer quite so ornamental.
Does a specially assigned ship's officer scan
the female personnel, alert for wrinkles or a sagging bum?
Do they go quietly, unasked, but warned by instinct
like elephants did (when there were elephants):
or screaming, bundled out the airlock
while the camera's elsewhere?

It will remain a mystery, like Dr Who's toilet.
But better to kill them, Captain. Or else one day,
an angry maenad-horde of beautiful old women
will storm your bridge, knowing exactly where
to pull your plug out.

The Sex Life of Slugs

Slugs make a civilised business of mating.
Each one both male and female,
    they come together side by side.
A fat white rope joins them, an umbilicus
    through which
they exchange genetic material.
Both lay eggs, a pearly caviar.

Slugs do not have, take or possess;
they build bridges between two equals,
share their twin-sexed selves.

If only we could share so easily
the male and female in us with our lovers;
the penetrating and the child-bearing
keep pulling us apart.

Meanwhile, after dark,
slugs stroll the pavements
    fearless of rape.

Christmas Island

He had no smell
although he never washed
(occasionally put Omo in the bath,
and got in, with his socks on)
and sweated in the hot sun, scrambling
over the cliffs, his dangerous old shotgun
pointing over his shoulder.
Thin, almost toothless, brown, with grizzly beard
and ape's bright, pushed-in eyes,
his bedroom carpeted with dust and filthy dishes
and suitcases of antique pornography,
(he added instruments of torture with a biro)
kept fit on fags, sugar and strong coffee,
he had no smell at all; we put it down
to Christmas Island, where he was irradiated
in the atom tests. Others got cancers, he
was preserved, like a supermarket strawberry
with a long shelf-life and no taste.

He told us, "The Americans got goggles. We
were told, cover your eyes. I could see
all the bones in my hand when it went off."

But he had no chance of Government compensation
for loss of body odour and a hand x-ray
branded onto his retina.

41

The Hip-bone's Connected to the Head-stone ...

"I've got a man's pelvis," she said. Like
a trophy dusted on the mantelpiece,
a possession marking her out
for special attention at the ante-natal.

Once it would have been her death;
encoded in her genes even as she struggled
to be born, wondered who to marry,
if her first would be a boy or girl.
Then days of agony and hope,
the baby strangled in its torque of bone,
her name alone on the headstone.

Now her baby swells, like
a fistful of peas soaked in a jar
with no way out.
Soon its blind head will push
at the too-small door –
but she laughs over coffee,
trusting the man with the knife
to deliver her.

Toothache, Heartache

My dentist has left me.
She called me by my name each time,
      without consulting notes.
She said my teeth were beautiful,
and gave me all the credit for it.
I felt beautiful and clever
      each time I left her.

When nothing needed doing, I shared her joy;
when something did, she ached with the pain
      her skill denied me.

Then she was gone, without a word.
Efficient young men manhandle my teeth
      lovelessly now.

But I remember her
encircling my head with dedicated fingers,
her legs around my chair
as if about to play a cello.

Bones from a Medic's Dustbin

I hold this human spine like a rosary of bone,
fingering the winged vertebrae.
I stack them to nest snugly
in totem poles of little trolls;
spread them to examine
the delicate neck rings,
the beaky thoracic vertebrae
which held the ribs, the massive
cushions of the lumbar bones
which carried, strained and ached,
and the shield-shaped pelvic bone
like the head of a knobby snake.

I fit it to my body all the way up;
at least my size, and closer to me now
than ever lovers were. But all my touching
of this body's stem can't tell me
whether man or woman, young or old,
but I can guess, poor, and probably Third World,
dark as their bones are milky
like white Aero. Western skeletons
cannot be bought and sold.

I think of this spine cocked to one side
to hoist a child, bent under hot, hard work,
twisted by pain, stretched out in sleep
and hope that once some fingers counted
the bumps in the living back, gently as mine do now.

Celebrating Raspberries

Bees fumble the raspberries
which relax their sour green knots;
flushing, engorging, hanging soft and heavy
to drip from their white wicks
and bleed warm into my hands.

Picking them, I could melt
into the lit-green canes and give myself
to that slow, sweet fruition, feel
the furred caress of bees
through every branch and berry
of my sun-swelled body.

Haiku

Swifts scream in circles
    swung on invisible wires
scouring the hot sky

*

Bee on dandelion –
    a black pupil burned into
the sun's yellow eye

*

Sudden red squirrel
    braced on the bark – a flame,
a flicker, then – gone

*

Sunset melts butter
    on the sea – sliced by a knife
of silver moonlight

*

Dead tree stumps in rows:
    one live twig raises
a slim green hand

The Sound of Snow in Summer

Every day the crunch of tyres on snow
splinters my sleep. I wake, year round,
to the fog of cold on the window, knowing
behind the blind, with its silver blackout film,
the street is glazed and gagged, the cars
humbly feeling their way, shrinking
from the give beneath them like people
treading on cockroaches:
though it's summer, though I've seen,
when I'm up early or he's late, the paper boy
skate by on roller blades that crackle
like crushed ice, still the dry, bright street
seems the contradiction,
still I wake to tyres on snow.

Mother Tongue

We all hate it when our mothers spit on a hanky,
dab at our faces to remove a harmless smudge. We
squirm and shy, appalled by intimacy which seems
somehow a threat: and they persist, curiously intent
on marking us with their saliva, invisible but indelible
despite our rubbing fist. We do it to our children,
all the same, licking them into shape as did our ancestors,
a baptism that claims them, though they rear, and toss
their heads, as horses fear the bridle; and we persist,
in a different kind of fear.

Milk

Dumpy skittles, set down in clumps
by the milkman,
they go down one by one.
My son is kept safe
by white magic,
     and my stupid faith.

A pint of milk a day!
I watch it down his bobbing throat,
     transfusion of liquid bone.
I measure his growth in empty bottles,
seeing his bones lengthen
stealthy as stalagmites
with their daily salting of calcium;
needing to feel I'm still feeding him
    as he grows away from me.

Dressing My Daughter

Dressing my dolls gave me a feeling,
a sleepy satisfaction –
I would tie and retie their sashes,
to keep the feeling there.

Now, dressing my daughter, I
give myself this pleasure
generously. My fingers feel the plush
of warm, clean cotton as I
smooth the vest over her fat beauty,
pop
her sparring hands through armholes,
tuck, and fasten, and twitch straight.
I pull on the socks, slide
her feet into her shoes, feel
the phut! as her heel fits home,
as I sing, chant, tickle, and make her smile.

Something old and simple holds me,
nothing to do with her or me,
or how much we love each other.
I think of Victorian gardeners
putting pears into muslin bags
while still on the trees –
storing something precious, making it safe.

Bell-buoy, Port of Tyne

A smooth mellow sound
spreads over the dark water
like cream on coffee;
the slow, sad tolling
of a sea-swung bell.

Watching the green cage, gull-bleached,
gently rocking,
lolling its bronze tongue
to the beat of engines
as boats skirt safely by;

I think of a long-drowned village,
its church bell rolling
with the waves, calling, calling
with the voice of the sea.

The sound draws us, nostalgic
for a world we don't remember,
makes us sad without knowing why:
the sad, slow tolling
of a sea-swung bell.

The Queen's Toilet

There's a bit of the Queen's toilet
    hanging in our hall.

She was due to visit the shipyards,
a duty call on a dying relative
    who's past eating grapes.
A discreet nudge from the Palace:
"She'll need special facilities, of course.
Unthinkable Her Majesty should share...!"

So they built, instead of the mighty metal
ships they had the muscle for,
a little sentry box of butter-smooth
    new wood
for the Royal convenience.
    No time to paint it, and just as well.

The Queen came and went, but
didn't go;
the shiny white plumbing, posh pink paper
stayed immaculate.
    They pulled it down again. The wood
walked off, some to make picture frames,
    leaving the shipyards
    to rust in peace.

"Your Great-Grandma would have been good at Maths"

Slice after slice, she has dished up her sleep to them,
keeping only the smallest piece for herself.
Now, tiredness keeps her warm, like fur.
    She's up before dawn, alone,
to make a shirt before breakfast
or there will be no dinner. A simple daily sum.

Small dead sighs from the just-cold range;
white linen gathers the light, and makes it gleam.
    She warms her eyes at it.
Her thickened fingers barely feel the needle
as it slips like a fish through the cloth –
tiny stitches unroll in hundreds, like eggs
    piped from a queen bee's sting.

Obedient as ironing, the shirt takes shape.
Into it, she sews her thirteen children
her man's shipyard thirst for beer
his rages and spent wage packets
and strangely, her luxury, numbers,
dancing through the needleholes in daisychains;
playing their tricks like toddlers in her head
    as she knocks back bread,
    hefts steaming sheets from the copper,
    leads the range with silver black.

Upstairs, bairns call, his braces drag
on floorboards. The shirt is finished,
fit for man to wear and woman to wash.
Her child, my grandma, takes it,
runs down the road for the money;
her survival, then her twins', then
my luxurious education, and
my children's choice-filled lives:

    while she begins her working day.

Ann More: Mrs John Donne

I thought myself a lucky woman then –
to capture such a poet, such a lover,
so skilful with his hands, his tongue, his pen...
I, his America, he, eager to discover.
A secret marriage; his imprisonment,
his risked career, and all for love of me!
I little knew my long confinement
would end too soon – released at thirty-three.
But babies came, twelve times I waxed and waned.
While he would beg the unruly sun stand still,
I prayed in secret to the moon, complained
of headache, backache, feeling tired and ill.
In one black year, a son and daughter died;
the child inside me kicked me as I cried.

Oh, I did love him, but the easy pleasure
two lovers in one bed, one mind, enjoy
popped like that saucy flea; instead, I'd measure
the long, slow, swollen months to girl or boy.
And he did love me, always, bride and mother,
despite the distorted shape his love had filled.
Only his God could take my place, no other,
when I and my last child his love had killed.
I know mine is a woman's common story;
but would have liked to share the acclaim he won,
lived longer, seen my children's growth, his glory –
a lucky woman, though my life was Donne.
But he gave to poems, I to babies, breath:
his labour brought him fame, mine brought me death.

On the Stepping Machine

a treadmill
designed to waste
labour and time
she's moving fast nowhere
at unchanging speed
knees rising and falling
as she scales giant's stairs
hair bouncing as she climbs
flight after flight of fancy
thin arms angled on the rails
buttocks in see-through lace
sexlessly perfect (despite the tattoo)
as she pounds up
a Himalayan skyscraper
her face blank, immobile,
not flushed, no panting,
ten, twenty, more minutes,
something is dripping
sweat gathering, ticking,
from each wrist, an oilspill
that marks time,
that leaves on the floor
twin puddles of her.

Pink High Heels

Seven years old, but almost new,
my sugar-pink shoes that once
closed round my feet
like firm, strong hands.
Narrow heels that tensed
the backs of my calves, made my walk
frivolous, impractical, but full
of power, tapping out my sex code
on the pavement.

They're in a drawer, bloomed with dust
like the skin of a marshmallow. My feet
reject them, being no longer shoe-shaped,
but in different ways.
The high-arched right shrinks and shies
from their friendly pressure,
neurotic; the rigid left
will not submit to enter, will not give
an inch. I can't wear them,
nor bear to be rid of them.

Crawl

The water takes me, and
I'm strong and beautiful, sleek
and pitiless as a shark, exulting
in my horizontal dance.
My reaching arms climb the lengths,
swerving round the other swimmers,
poor ice-bergs! I think, enjoying
my own arrogance.

One mile later, drunk on water,
I struggle out, a damaged dragonfly
out of its chrysalis.
Reach for my stick,
limp painfully on mis-matched legs,
"that poor girl."
The little mermaid swapped her tail
for feet like mine.

No prince is worth it, pet,
believe me.

April Fools

A long way from my North-East coast,
this sepia seaside bungalow in Kent;
where Uncle, ninety-seven, hugs me tight
to say that we are linked.
Both April Fools, feet shattered on the same day
sixty-nine years apart:
mine by a Ford Sierra
his by a German shell.
I smell his old man's suit
as we stand toe to toe
in matching Reeboks.

I bought him those for comfort
but his daily shirt and tie
keep standards up.

He's always done his duty.
First the Great War, then a wife
whose Nerves became his children;
when she died, a senile sister...
now alone, no longer ordered over the top,
he's allowed to be
wonderful for his age.

He's not fooled – knows who to blame
for the shuffling, old man's feet
he's had since twenty, but
can only snipe with words
at an enemy, safely entrenched,
who has forgotten him.

Trench Experience
(Imperial War Museum)

In darkness we walked through
the rats, the blam and thud of shells,
the mud walls made of resin.
Young men in effigy spoke endlessly
on tape loops
reading letters home, calling for help,
ignoring us, as if we were the ghosts.

And so we were. No mud stuck to our shoes.
Our clothes were dry, no seeping corpses
reeked – just a faint miasma, like Elsan.
There was no fear.
Moved, impressed, gasping for tea,
we headed for clean toilets and
shockingly priced cakes.

They couldn't have done it better,
without putting the tourists off. Fair's fair.

But Uncle, when we visited next day,
flooded it for us with his memories.
The guilt of being still alive and whole
when all your friends are dead or
shot apart. Knowing you are next.
His third time into battle, his lost gun,
his bleeding into mud for hours and hours:
being kept alive on drops of best champagne,
less precious then than water.

Fantasy

A prick of fantasy comes always
with a barb of guilt.
Lately I indulge in flash photos
of myself, luxuriously
old and alone. Just being.
Pegging down huge sheets of time
earning a cup of tea, a book,
by buying bread or pulling up a weed –
enjoying my aches on a full-time basis
with no-one to care for but me.

But I feel bad about it,
wiping out for split seconds
those I love so much
and needing such perverted comfort
when I ought to be lusting for
the golden limbs of beautiful young men.

Men Must Wear the Trousers

Old women's legs in winter
seem stick-bare between thick coats
and fur-lined boots,
the sharp wind whittling at the bone.

Faces clenched around their adopted teeth,
dreading the fall, the hip, the bedpan,
they stilt on,
crepe stockings where round muscle was;
brandishing their frozen shins,
to say,
      "We are still women."

Poets Don't

Poets don't buy shelves from MFI
or have extensions built upon their houses;
poets don't kiss, and then not tell, or spend
their lives being secretly faithful to their spouses.

Poets can be waspish, but not WASPS
(unless they've been to Oxford, that's alright);
avoid being in majorities, and better not
be middle class, provincial, that's a blight.

It's fine to be North-Eastern (and a miner),
it's fine to be suburban (and go mad);
it's good to live in inner-city ghettoes
or on a mountain – Whitley Bay is bad.

A happy childhood's something best kept quiet.
I can pretend my respectable relatives are dead:
but I've no chance of being called a poet –
the world can see that I've got avenue-cred.

IRON Press was formed in Spring 1973, initially to publish the magazine IRON which more than two decades, and more than 1,500 writers on, survives as one of the country's most active alternative mags – a fervent purveyor of new poetry, fiction and graphics. £12.00 gets you a subscription. Try our intriguing book list too, titles which can rarely be found on the shelves of mega-stores. Fortified by a belief in good writing, as against literary competitions or marketing trivia, IRON remains defiantly a small press. Our address is on the second page of this book